In the year 55 BC, a Roman general called Julius Caesar
looked across the English Chan[nel] [at the shores]
of Britain. He'd heard there wer[e things he]
needed — grain for food and met[al.] [He decided]
to invade and see for himself.

Caesar had sent messengers ahead telling
the local people, the Celts, of his plan. He hoped
they would surrender without a fight.

No way!

Tell your master we will defend ourselves!

Caesar sailed across the Channel with his army, but when
the Romans fought the Celts there was no clear winner.
Caesar went away, but the next year he returned with many
more troops, won a battle and took away **hostages**.

A hundred years passed before the Romans
returned to Britain again. This time they
conquered most of the local **tribes**.
The Romans settled in Britain
and began to build forts,
towns and roads.

Put on your armour

If you wanted to be a soldier in the Roman army you had to be at least 170 centimetres tall and not less than 18 years old. You had to have a strong, well-built body and good eyesight. An army doctor checked your health and then you swore an **oath** of loyalty to the Emperor.

Soldiers did a lot of training to make themselves strong and fit. They swam across rivers, dug trenches, chopped down trees and climbed over **obstacles**.

Gasp!

Soldiers were expected to march for long periods wearing their armour and carrying all their kit.

The full kit

helmet

pole to carry kit on shoulder

scarf to stop chainmail chafing the skin

chainmail tunic

cloth tunic

cooking pot, clothes, blanket and food

dagger

javelin

sword

leather skirt

painted shield in protective leather cover

leather sandals with metal studs on soles

After a day's march, the soldiers made camp. They got together to build fires and cook their food. The soldiers slept in tents made of goatskin with eight men in each tent.

Meet the locals

In Britain, the land was divided up between many Celtic tribes and each tribe had a leader or king. The people wore clothes made from checked or striped material. **Warriors** tattooed their bodies. Both men and women liked fine jewellery.

For much of the time the people lived peacefully as farmers. They grew wheat, barley and vegetables in their fields. They got meat, wool, milk and leather from their farm animals.

house on an island

bridge

6

The Celtic warriors were skilled at making weapons. They attacked their enemies on fast, light **chariots**. They liked to take the heads of their enemies home as trophies!

As fighting sometimes broke out between the tribes, their houses needed some protection. Some houses were built on islands in lakes or lochs. Others were built on the tops of hills, surrounded by ditches and fences.

hill fort →

7

Get a lifestyle

When the Romans came to Britain they found the tribes treated them in different ways. Some tribes were **hostile** and often attacked the Romans. Other tribes were friendly. They knew that if they **co-operated** with the Romans, the Romans would protect them from their enemies.

There were other benefits for the Celts if they helped the Romans. They could improve their lifestyle by selling things like grain or precious metals such as silver and tin to the Romans. The Romans admired the Celts' skill at making metal objects such as weapons and other beautifully decorated items.

When the Romans set up local councils to collect taxes
and keep law and order, many Celtic chieftains joined them.

After a while, the Celts and Romans lived in peace.
Many Celts began to dress like Romans and follow their
customs and habits. Some grew rich and were able to live
in Roman-style houses. A lot of people we think of as
Romans were actually Celts.

Take to the road

The Celts travelled around on winding paths and dirt tracks.
The Romans needed to move troops about the country quickly
so they created a new network of good roads. They had to be
strong enough to carry heavy carts. They were paved with flat
stones and ran in straight lines with as few bends as possible.

Every thousand paces there was a stone at the side of the road. The Roman word for thousand is *mille* and so that is where the word *milestone* comes from.

If you wanted something to eat or drink, you stopped at a roadside tavern.

If you wanted to stop overnight, there were guest houses near the road.

bullock cart carrying a heavy load

farmer

If you were a road engineer you used a piece of equipment called a groma to help you find the straightest, flattest route.

large stones placed in a trench
layer of smaller stones
gravel

the road surface:
flat stones or cobbles

The Romans built around 2,000 miles of roads linking important towns, sea ports and army camps. Some of today's roads such as the A2 from London to Dover and the A5 from London to Chester run along the same routes as Roman roads.

soldiers

wealthy lady being carried in a litter

chariot carrying government letters

Mix some cement

If you were an Ancient Roman, you may well have mixed a lot of cement. The Romans discovered how to make cement which they used to stick bricks and stone together. They invented the arch which was a very strong way of holding up a roof. So, using arches and cement, they were able to build much bigger buildings than ever before.

Arches were used to make bridges over valleys and rivers.

An aqueduct was a channel which brought water to a town.

Roman towns were designed with streets going in a criss-cross pattern. In the middle of the town there was always a forum – a market place. Besides houses and blocks of flats, there were many grand public buildings.

A basilica was a large hall used for courts of law and council meetings.

A temple was where Romans worshipped one of their gods.

The thermae were public baths where citizens could wash and relax.

An amphitheatre was where public entertainments – like gladiator fights – took place.

Impressive arches were built at the entrance to a town or to celebrate a battle.

13

STAGE 7

Shop till you drop

Roman towns were very busy places. Often, carts were banned from the centre of town during the day as they created traffic jams. If you were a delivery man, you might have to do your deliveries at night. The streets had pavements and good drains.

baker's shop

cobbler's workshop

Portia loves Marcus

street sweeper

stepping stones for crossing the road

14

There were rows of shops in the streets as well as market stalls. If you were a Roman child who was lucky enough to go to school, you may have sat in the baker's shop. Often, pupils had their lessons in the corner of a shop or even in the street.

There were fountains at street corners where people collected their water. There were plenty of public toilets as only the very rich had bathrooms in their houses.

posters advertising next gladiator fight

cushion shop

pupils having a school lesson: canvas screens gave some privacy

fruit stall

important lawyer with slaves to carry his papers

fountain

15

Stay fit

If you were a Roman with some time to spare, you might want to visit the exercise yard at the local public baths. Most Romans, both men and women, liked to work up a sweat because they believed it helped to purify their bodies.

If running about didn't appeal to you, you could still work up a sweat by lying in the sunbathing area.

Roman sports

running with a hoop

gymnastics

training with weights

throwing the discus

Wrestlers and boxers were professional sportsmen so they took training seriously. Boxers might spend a lot of time thumping a punch bag.

Wrestlers rubbed wax or oil into their skin to keep it supple, then covered themselves in dust so they could get a better grip on each other.

Trigon was a favourite ball-throwing game for three players.
Some lazy people brought a slave to pick the ball up off the ground for them.

STAGE 9

Soak away your cares

Once you had worked up a good sweat, you went and washed it off in the bath house. Public baths were very important to Romans and some were to be found in huge buildings decorated with statues and paintings.

The baths weren't just places to wash away the cares of the day. People met friends there, exchanged gossip or discussed business. There were separate baths for men and women.

You paid to get into the baths.

Two, please.

There was a shop where you could buy towels and perfumed oils.

It was wise to pay a slave to keep an eye on your clothes in case someone stole them from the changing room.

There were three types of bath. You usually used the caldarium first, which was very hot and steamy.

You could have a massage here.

Next, you went into the tepidarium, which was warm and relaxing.

Romans didn't use soap. They covered their bodies in oil then scraped off the oil - along with the dirt - using a metal scraper called a strigil.

Lastly, you plunged into the frigidarium, which was cold and refreshing.

Huge boilers were used to keep the water hot and the rooms heated. Large quantities of water were brought into the baths by aqueducts.

Milk a goat

After the Roman invasion of Britain, most of the local people still lived in the countryside on small farms. If you were a wealthy Roman you could afford a big house and lots of land. As there were no tractors, oxen and donkeys did the hard work.

Oxen pulled ploughs and heavy carts.

Donkeys carried things on their backs or were used to turn flour mills or thresh grain.

Sheep were kept for milk and wool.

Goats gave milk and hair for ropes and sacks.

Pork from pigs was the Romans' favourite meat.

Meat, eggs and feathers for pillows came from hens, ducks and geese.

Farms grew vegetables and fruit to supply the nearby towns.

cabbages

leeks

radishes

beans

onions

apples

lettuces

pears

garlic

Romans ate and drank large quantities of grapes, wine, olives and olive oil. These things didn't grow well in Britain so they were brought in on ships from warmer countries.

While the Romans enjoyed a comfortable lifestyle in the countryside, the Celts often had to work for them on their farms. It was a hard life and there was a lot of hunger and disease.

21

Choose your room

A Celt family slept, cooked, worked and played in one big room – their hut. If you were a wealthy Roman, you had a house with many rooms. A town house was called a domus. A country house was called a villa. The houses were usually built round a **courtyard** with a garden.

Some houses had central heating. A **furnace** at one end created hot air which flowed through the house in a space under the floor.

The houses had living rooms, dining rooms, a kitchen and bedrooms. Water came in pipes to the bathroom.
If you were a well-read Roman, you had a library.

There were couches, chairs and stools to sit on. Belongings were stored in cupboards or chests. The rooms were lit by oil lamps and there were charcoal **braziers** to heat you if the weather was chilly.

Writing was done on wax tablets or papyrus (paper) scrolls.

shelf for books and letters

cupboard

lamp

couch

pens and ink

writing paper

brazier

strong chest for valuables

lamp

STAGE 12

Mix up some paint

If you were a Roman artist you did a lot of house painting. The Romans liked the walls of their rooms to be brightly decorated. Firstly, the walls were covered in wet plaster, then the artist painted on to the plaster before it dried. This meant the paintings lasted a long time. They were called frescoes.

Paintings of landscapes, birds, fruit and flowers were popular.

Sometimes, the owners had their portraits painted on the walls.

The most important rooms in the house usually had **mosaic** floors. The floors were covered in wet plaster, then little pieces of stone were pressed into it. The pieces of stone were laid in simple patterns, but if you had money to spare, you could have pictures of things.

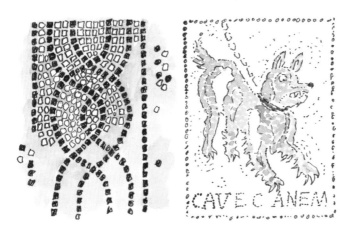

This mosaic says:
Beware of the dog!

CAVE CANEM

Rooms and gardens were decorated with statues. They were made of marble or metal, then painted.

25

Twirl in your toga

If you were a Roman you probably slept in your underclothes. For men, that was a loincloth and for women, something like a bikini. All Romans put a short tunic on over their underclothes. Women sometimes wore a longer dress called a stola and wrapped themselves in a palla when going out.

belt→

palla→

In colder climates, people wore cloaks trimmed with fur. Men, including soldiers, wore trousers.

leather sandal ↓

boot ↓

a soldier's shoe with nails in the sole for long marches

A toga was a thin woollen blanket which was wrapped around your body over your tunic. It was hot, heavy and awkward to wear so it was kept for special occasions.

Men visited the barber's shop to have a shave and catch up with the gossip. Shaving was painful as the barbers didn't use soap.

Ouch!

Wealthy women spent a long time putting on their make-up and having their hair done. They sometimes wore wigs made of hair cut from slaves.

Children wore the same clothes as grown-ups. They wore a *bulla* round their necks - a lucky charm to ward off evil spirits.

Munch on a meatball

If you were an ordinary Roman, your meals were quite simple. People who lived in the country cooked their food over a fire. Town houses often didn't have kitchens so food was bought ready-made from shops.

Milk was only drunk by children.

bread

porridge

vegetables

sometimes meat

Rich people had large kitchens in their houses and a bakehouse for making bread. They liked to have grand dinner parties where guests lay on couches as they ate and were entertained by musicians.

28

Dinner had three courses.

MENU

Starters: salad with lettuce, radishes, mushrooms, small fish, eggs and cheese

Main course: various kinds of meat, meatballs, fish and vegetables

Last course: fruit and nuts

It was difficult to keep food fresh in Roman times, so meat was covered in a rich sauce to hide any stale smell or flavour. Sometimes there were unusual dishes like rose pie or roasted flamingo tongues. The guests drank from glass cups and ate from silver plates.

Tinkle your tambourine

Musicians, dancers and acrobats often performed while wealthy people were eating. If you were an ordinary Roman you probably enjoyed a good song or a dance accompanied by a flute and drum.

twin pipes   tambourine and rattle   lyre   flute   cymbals   trumpet

Gambling with dice was a popular pastime.

Oh Goddess Fortuna, bring me luck!

People played games like draughts with the grid scratched on the ground.

30

Children played with dolls made of cloth, wood or clay. They also had kites, spinning tops, seesaws and swings. Wealthy parents might give their children a little chariot, which could be pulled by geese.

Woah!

Romans liked watching stage plays. They built theatres, which could seat thousands of people. The actors performed in front of painted scenery, wearing brightly-coloured masks which could be easily seen from a distance.

seats: poor people at the back, rich people at the front

stage

Remember to bring a cushion to sit on!

31

STAGE 16

Free a slave

Most Romans owned a slave or two, unless they were very poor. Rich people had dozens of slaves to do tasks around the house, farm or workplace. Slaves came from all corners of the Roman Empire. They were bought and sold in market places where they had to wear a sign round their necks advertising their skills.

The letters "FUG", meaning fugitive, were branded on a slave if he'd tried to escape.

FUG

reliable strong has done farm work

good with children

can read and write

Some slave owners treated their slaves kindly but other owners were very cruel. Slaves who worked in the mines or on building sites had the hardest life and suffered from disease and injury.

Greek slaves were expensive because they were educated and skilful. Most schoolteachers were Greek slaves.

Some slaves could read and write and became secretaries or ran businesses for their owners. These slaves were usually paid and if they saved enough money they could buy their freedom. If you wished, you could give freedom to a slave who had served you well. After a short **ceremony**, the slave was given a special hat as a mark of freedom.

33

STAGE 17

Cheer on your team

If you were a wealthy businessman you might own a team of **charioteers**. Chariot racing was a very popular Roman sport. The races were held on a circular race track called a circus. On race day, thousands of fans wearing their team colours came to cheer on their club.

There were things to buy before going into the circus...

entrance tokens

snacks and drink

a cushion to sit on

souvenirs of your favourite charioteer or horses

Racing chariots were made of wood and **wickerwork** and were very light. Charioteers wore their team colours and protective leather clothing.

leather → helmet

Horses' reins were tied round the waist so hands were free

waistcoat

Knife to cut reins if there was an accident

leg protectors

The race began when the starter dropped a handkerchief and lasted seven laps. Charioteers were young slaves. The most skilful were treated like celebrities and earned lots of money, but racing was dangerous and many died young.

← A bronze dolphin was lifted from a stand after each lap.

Give a gift to a god

Both the Romans and the Celts believed in many gods.
The Celts didn't build temples but worshipped their gods in
special places – like a clearing in the middle of a wood or on
a river bank. People threw valuable objects, like swords and
jewellery, into lakes and bogs. They hoped these would please
the gods who would grant them their wishes – perhaps
recovery from an illness or victory in battle.

The Celts had
priests called
Druids.
They carried
out religious
ceremonies.

They killed
animals – and
sometimes humans –
so that their
blood could be
offered to
the gods.

36

The Romans built magnificent temples for their gods where people could go to pray or leave gifts. On certain days, parades and festivals were held in honour of the gods.

a Roman temple with altar where animals were sacrificed for the gods

Romans prayed at home, too. Every house had a little shrine where gifts of food and wine were left for the gods.

a household shrine

Some Roman gods:
Jupiter and Juno, king and queen of the gods

Venus, goddess of beauty

Mars, god of war

Neptune, god of the sea

STAGE 19

Beware of Boudica

If you were a Roman soldier in Britain you might be called on to keep the locals under control. Some Celtic tribes didn't like being bossed around by the Romans. When King Pratusagus of the Iceni tribe died, the Romans took over his land and flogged his wife, Queen Boudica. Boudica was described as a wild-looking woman with long red hair down to her hips and wearing clothes of many colours.

Boudica decided to teach the Romans a lesson. Riding in her chariot at the head of her army, she led her troops to the Roman town of Colchester. She burned the town to the ground and killed most of the Romans who lived there. Then she did the same to the towns of London and St Albans. Thousands of Romans were killed.

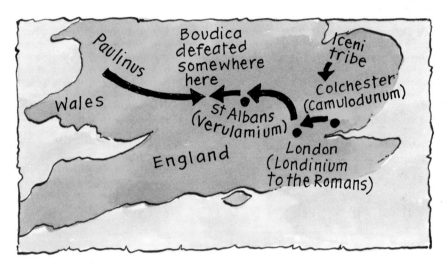

Paulinus, the Roman leader in Britain, was in Wales at the time. He brought his army back quickly to face Boudica. The Celtic warriors were no match for the **disciplined** Roman soldiers, and 80,000 men in Boudica's army were killed.

It's said that Boudica drank poison rather than be caught by the Romans.

STAGE 20

Put up some walls

The Romans had trouble from the locals in the north, too. Scottish tribes often attacked the Romans. The Romans found it difficult to track down these warriors in the mountains and glens.

The Romans came up with a solution – a wide, long wall. The wall stretched right across the north of England from coast to coast. There were camps for the soldiers along the wall as well as **fortified** gates. This allowed the Romans to control who passed in and out and keep an eye on the northern tribes.

Towns often grew up outside the gates.
↓

The wall was called Hadrian's Wall after the Roman Emperor. If you were a Roman soldier, you probably hoped you weren't sent on a tour of duty at Hadrian's Wall. It was often cold, wet and snow-covered. Soldiers there wrote home for extra clothing.

Twenty years after building Hadrian's Wall, the Romans built another one further north. The Antonine Wall was built of turf with a wooden fence on top. It stretched across the middle of Scotland.

Say goodbye

For centuries, the Roman army kept the islands of Britain at peace but trouble was brewing. The huge Roman Empire was being invaded by enemies from all sides. The Romans didn't have enough soldiers to defend it. The east and south of Britain were attacked by warriors and pirates from the Angle and Saxon tribes across the North Sea.

The Romans built forts along the coast to try and fight off the invaders but in the year 410 AD the Roman Emperor decided the Romans could no longer keep an army in Britain. The soldiers were taken away and the Celtic people had to fend for themselves.

The Romans had been in Britain for around 460 years. They built roads, harbours, towns and villas. They brought new ideas, customs and language. The soldiers, officials and merchants who lived in Britain came from all parts of the Roman Empire – like Spain, North Africa, Egypt or the Middle East. Many settled down and decided to stay when the Roman army left.

However, as Britain was invaded by other people, the things the Romans left behind began to disappear.

If you were a Roman soldier in Britain, perhaps *you* were the very last one to step on to a ship and sail away. Perhaps you left some things behind which were discovered thousands of years later – some clues on how to be a Roman.

a hoard of money ↓

a shoe ↘

a good luck ↙ charm

a metal decoration ↗ from your horse harness

graffiti ↓

a ring ↘

horsehair plume from your helmet ↙

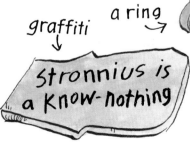

Stronnius is a know-nothing

a knife ↑

Glossary

boundary	the agreed edge of a piece of land
braziers	metal baskets which contain burning wood or coal, designed to heat a room
ceremony	a special, formal event governed by particular rules
charioteers	people who drive chariots
chariots	very fast two-wheeled horse-drawn carts, used in battle or for racing
co-operated	worked together
courtyard	a paved area outside, surrounded by walls or buildings
disciplined	obeying orders rather than being ruled by emotions
fortified	built to resist attack
furnace	a special oven made to hold a very hot fire
hostages	people who are held prisoner in order to force their friends and family to do something
hostile	warlike, aggressive
mosaic	a pattern made from squares of coloured stone
oath	a solemn promise
obstacles	objects that get in the way, making it difficult to move
papyrus	a kind of paper made from flattened reeds
thresh	beat wheat to release the edible grain
tribes	groups of people who come from the same place and have the same beliefs
warriors	soldiers
weapons	objects like swords, spears and knives, designed to wound people
wickerwork	twigs woven together into objects

Index

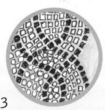

GALLERY OF GREAT ROMAN IDEAS

STRAIGHT, WELL-SURFACED ROADS

PUBLIC BATHS AND SPORTS FACILITIES

CEMENT — WHICH ALLOWED THEM TO MAKE ARCHES AND GRAND BUILDINGS

Ideas for reading

Written by Clare Dowdall PhD
Lecturer and Primary Literary Consultant

Learning objectives: identify and summarise evidence from a text to support a hypothesis; use knowledge of different organisational features of texts to find information effectively; interrogate texts to deepen and clarify understanding and response; listen to a speaker, make notes on the talk and use notes to develop a role-play

Curriculum links: History: Why have people invaded and settled in Britain in the past? A Roman case study

Interest words: braziers, charioteers, fortified, mosaic, papyrus, thresh, wickerwork

Resources: ICT, whiteboards, notebooks

Getting started

This book can be read over two or more guided reading sessions.

- In pairs, ask children to list three facts about the Romans to share with the rest of the group.

- Share facts and create a *What we know about the Romans* list. Use this list to raise questions that will guide reading, e.g. *What did the Romans like to wear?*

- As a group, look at the front and back covers. Help the children to infer information about the Romans based on the picture, e.g. *the men wore armour, the women wore jewellery.*

Reading and responding

- Read *Stage 1 Plan an invasion* to the children. Check that children understand the word *invasion.*

- Model how to make notes about the invasion of Britain on a whiteboard. Talk the children through the process. Ask children to recount how and why Britain was invaded by the Romans to a partner.

- Ask children to select one question from the list generated, e.g. *What did the Romans like to wear?* Ask children to explain how they can locate information effectively.